T4-AKX-973

Babies are Angels

By Bonnie Altenhein

PHOTOGRAPHS BY BRUCE HENSON

PARK LANE PRESS
NEW YORK • NEW JERSEY

This 1996 edition is published by Park Lane Press,
a division of Random House Value Publishing, Inc.,
40 Engelhard Avenue, Avenel, New Jersey 07001.

Random House
New York • Toronto • London • Sydney • Auckland

Printed in Mexico

Book Design by Renato Stanisic

Library of Congress Cataloging-in-Publication Data
Altenhein, Bonnie.
Babies are angels / by Bonnie Altenhein ; photographs by Bruce Henson.
p. cm.
ISBN 0-517-20008-2
1. Infants—Quotations, maxims, etc. 2. Angels—Quotations, maxims, etc. 3. Infants—Pictorial works. I. Henson, Bruce. II. Title.
PN6084.I48A48 1996
305.23'2—dc20

95-43506
CIP

8 7 6 5 4 3 2 1

Introduction

It is said among those who know about miracles, that when the first baby laughed for the first time, on earth, the merry tinkle of baby laughter broke into a million teeney slivers and bits that went hopping and skipping and jumping about, and this miracle was the beginning of angels.

When you touch their silky smooth skin...when you feel their sweet baby kisses...you know you are close to the angels. When you listen to babies whisper secret gurgles and coos...when you smell their delicious baby smells... you know you are close to the angels. And when you see the enchantment and wonder shining in their eyes...when you know the joy of their unconditional trust and love...you know that all babies are angels, born to fulfill our most divine hopes and dreams...born to be the caretakers of our future.

Babies *are the angels' way of saying all's right with the world.*

A happy *childhood*

begins at the

moment of birth.

Babies *are special angels whose wings and halos get smaller as their arms, legs and lungs get stronger.*

Adorable *babies grow up to be whimsical adults.*

Babies *are just old people starting over.*

Guardian *angels*

watch over the world so

babies are safe to grow.

Look *gently to our babies; they are our hope for the future.*

Drool *happens.*

Babies *are a gentle reminder that an angel is nearby.*

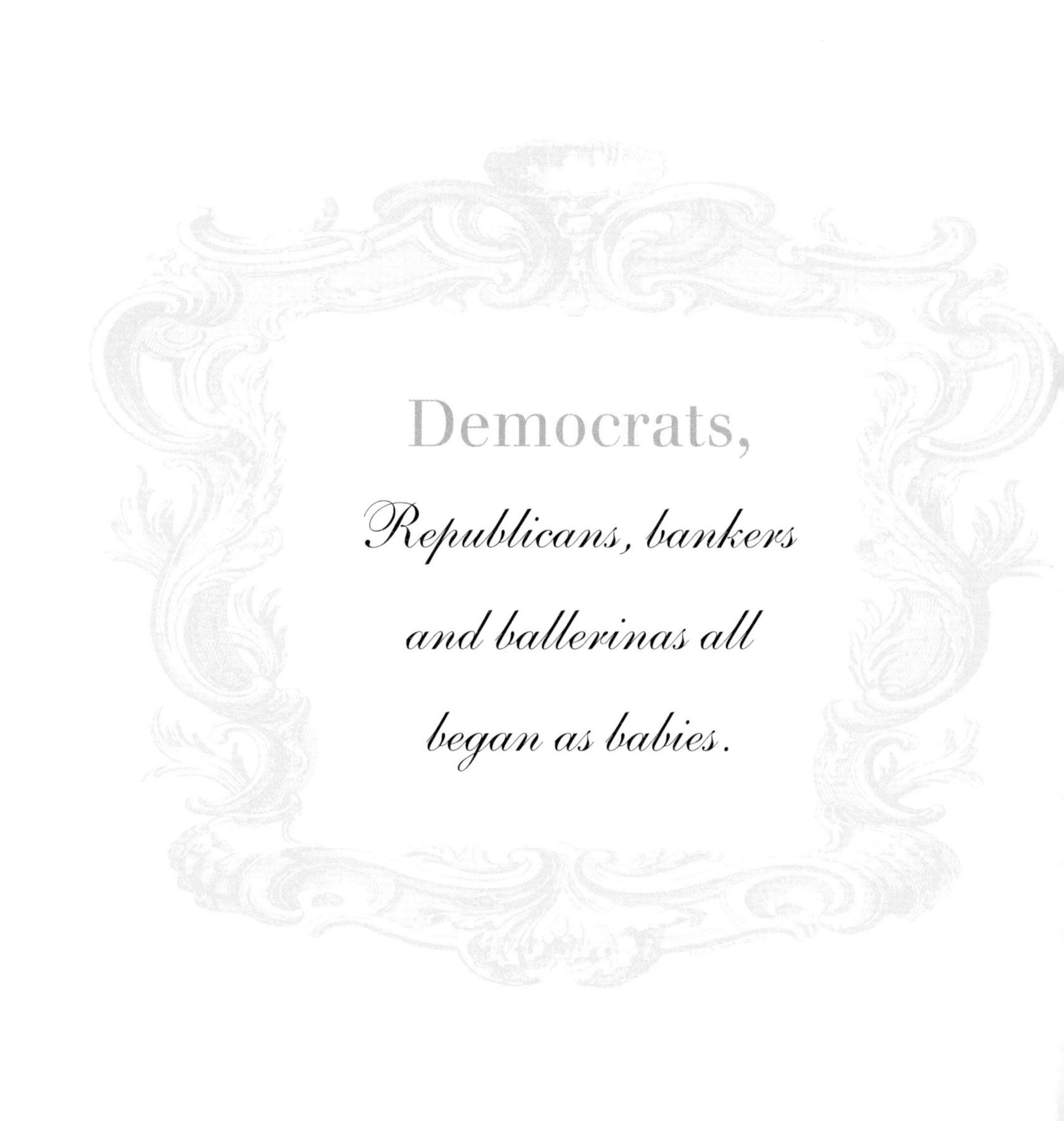

Democrats,

Republicans, bankers

and ballerinas all

began as babies.

Baby *talk is the language of love.*

Babies *are a divine message from God that the world should keep on keeping on.*

You're *never too old for a nap and a blankie.*

Babies *are the first lesson we learn in unconditional love.*

Babies *just want*

to have fun.

Carpe *disposable diapers!*

Angels *can't be everywhere, so God created babies.*

Babies *are*

little angels who reflect

the miraculous part

of ourselves.

Babies *sleep*
like angels and wake up
full of the devil.

When *in doubt, put it in your mouth.*

Baby *fat,*

wrinkles and rolls

show where smiles have

been in heaven.

STUFFed
animaL
Food

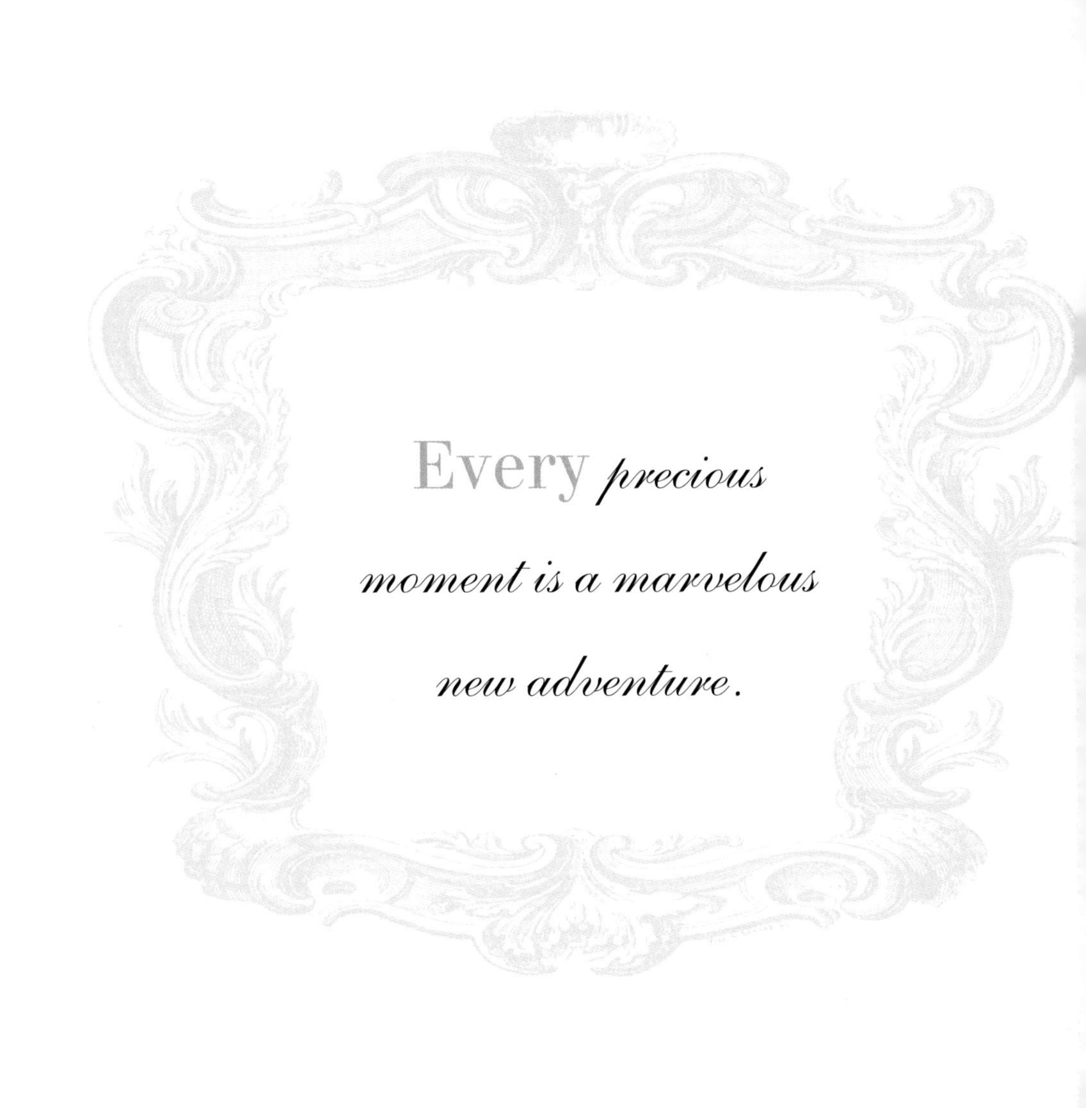

Every *precious*

moment is a marvelous

new adventure.

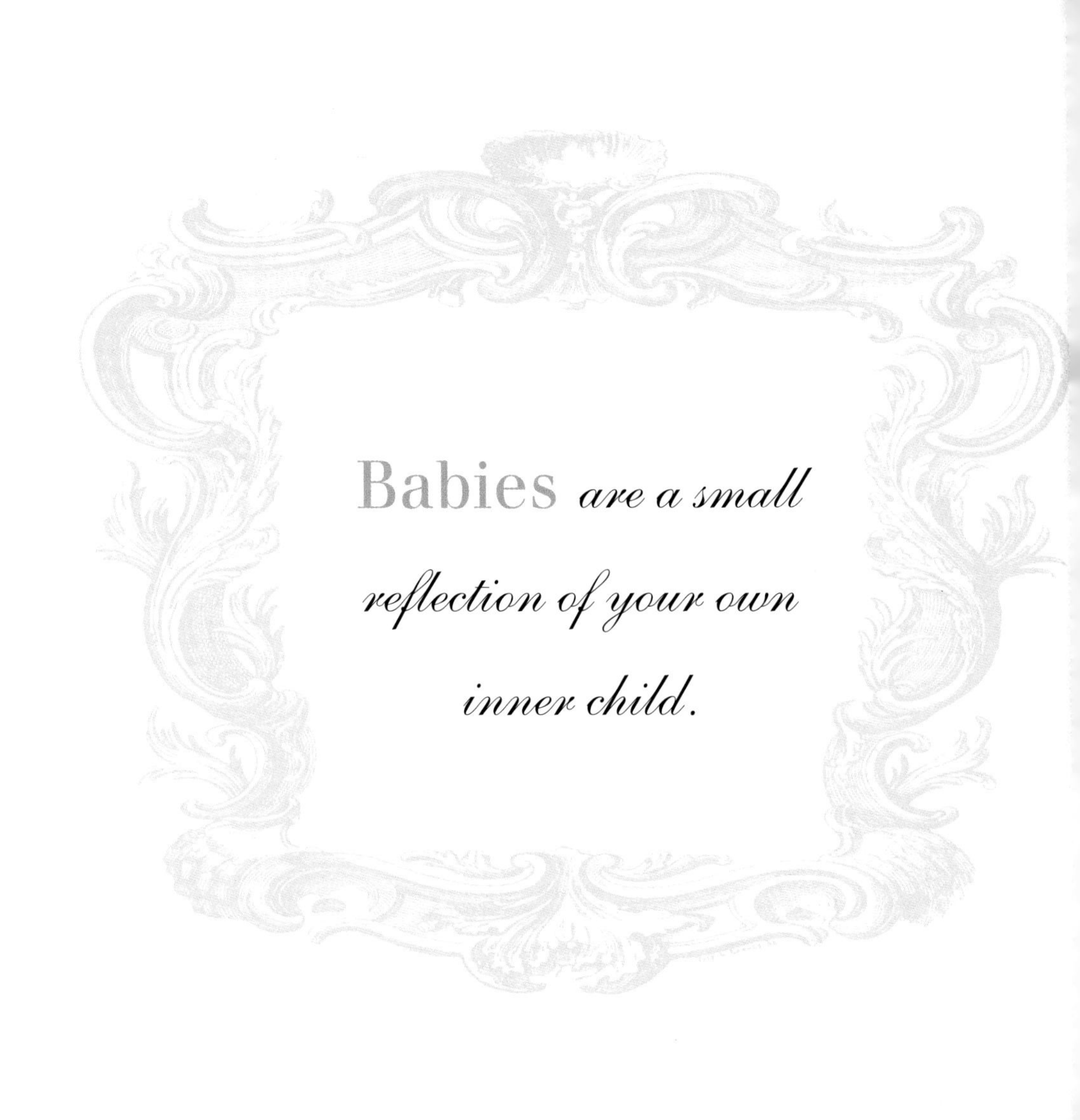

Babies *are a small reflection of your own inner child.*

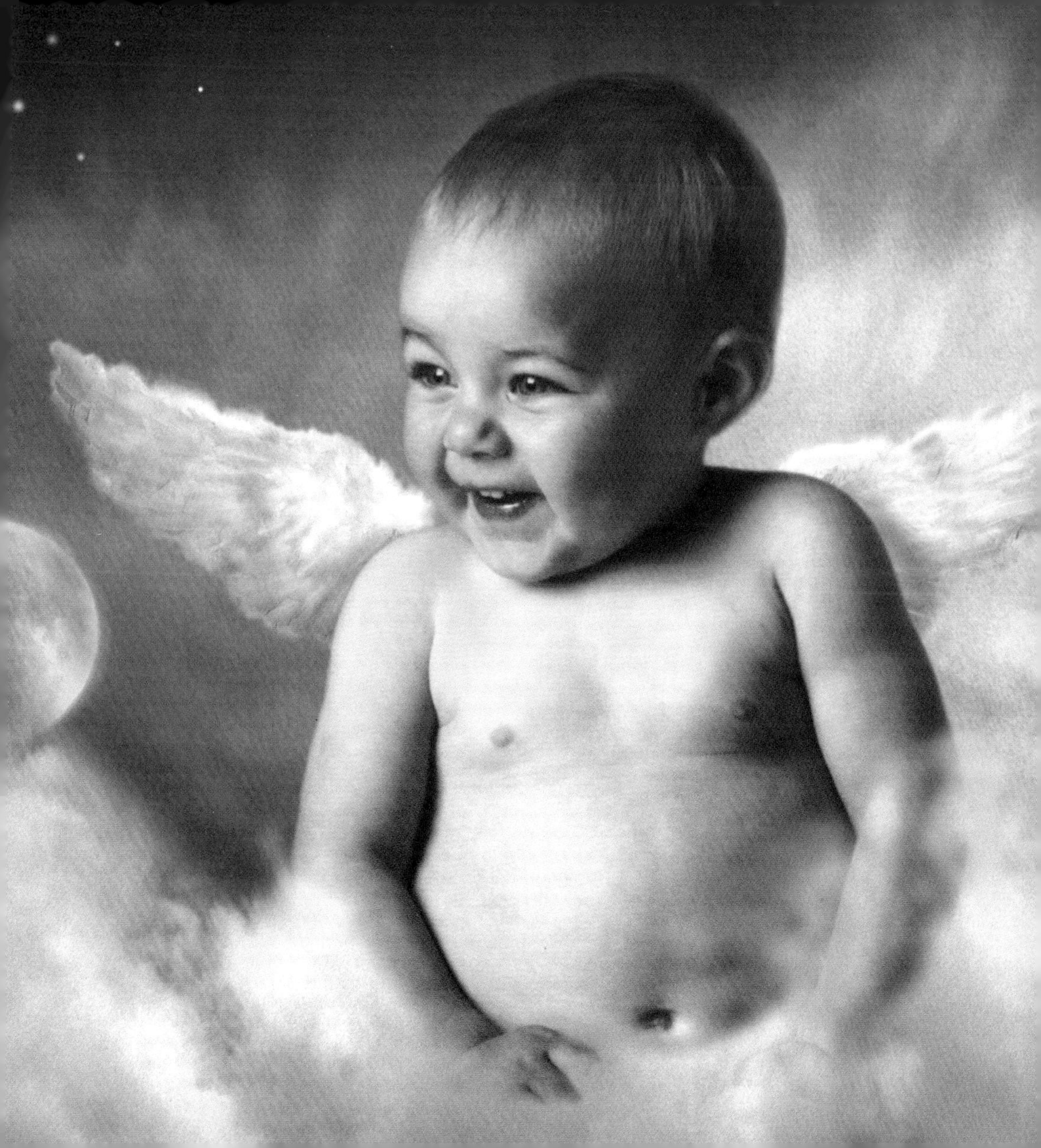

Let us *give our babies roots so they may grow strong, and wings so they may learn to fly.*

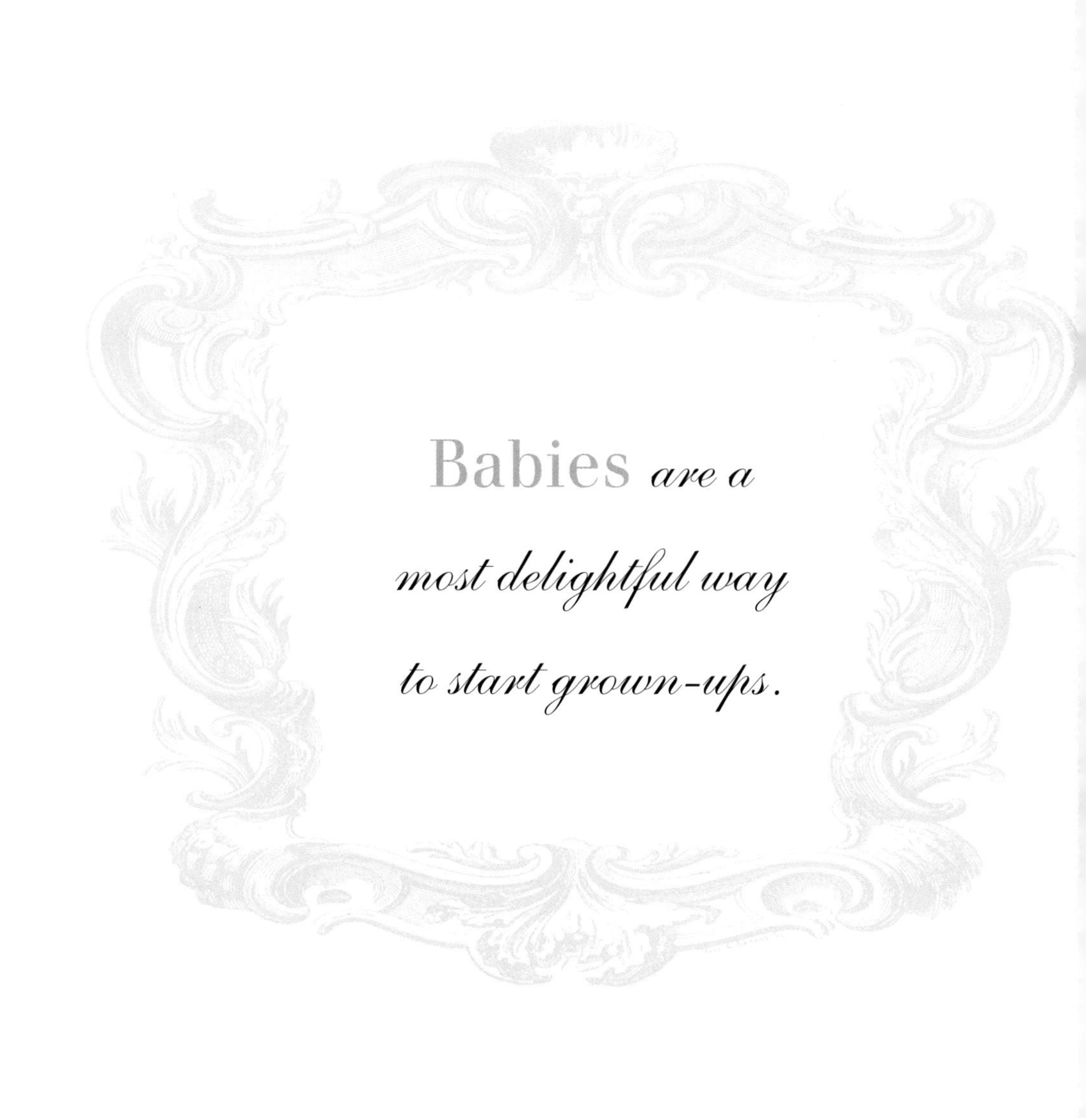

Babies *are a most delightful way to start grown-ups.*

Babies *are a divine affirmation of the wonder of life.*

Babies *are special angels who carry a little bit of heaven into the world with them.*

Babies *are*

the beginning of a

precious dream about

to come true.

A baby *who receives love, learns to give love in return.*

Don't *name*

your baby after a

Zen god, a rock star,

or anything that grows

in your garden.

Bonnie Altenhein has been writing about everything from angels to zebras since she was old enough to hold a crayon. She was born and raised in New York City, where she worked as editor of *Better Homes and Gardens* magazine, former secretary and "joke coordinator" for Joan Rivers, and creator of WATCH MY LIPS!, a unique, million-dollar company that developed a line of "greeting seed" cards that became an overnight industry phenomenon. She is the author of a best-selling calendar, poster, and several greeting cards featuring angels. Her previous books include *How Angels Get Their Wings, Christmas Angels, Angel Love, Moms Are Angels,* and *Santa's Angels.* She lives with her husband Gerry in Delray Beach, Florida.

Bruce E Henson spent three months taking pictures of seventy wiggling, giggling, screaming, wetting, and smiling angels while producing the images for this book. At the same time, he photographed every cloud, sunset, and moonscape that passed over his house. He also photographed the props that appear throughout the book. All photographs were then put together in the computer to complete each image. Mr. Henson is a graduate of The Art Center College of Design in Los Angeles, California. He is a partner in Northern Exposure Greeting Cards, a photographic card line. He lives with his wife Linda and their daughter Kelly in Sonoma County, California.